# ANIMAL RIGHTS

# PET RESCUE

Elsie Olson

Checkerboard
Library

An Imprint of Abdo Publishing
abdopublishing.com

# abdopublishing.com

Published by Abdo Publishing, a division of ABDO, PO Box 398166, Minneapolis, Minnesota 55439. Copyright © 2018 by Abdo Consulting Group, Inc. International copyrights reserved in all countries. No part of this book may be reproduced in any form without written permission from the publisher. Checkerboard Library™ is a trademark and logo of Abdo Publishing.

Printed in the United States of America, North Mankato, Minnesota
102017
012018

Design: Christa Schneider, Mighty Media, Inc.
Production: Mighty Media, Inc.
Editor: Megan Borgert-Spaniol
Cover Photographs: Shutterstock
Interior Photographs: AP Images, p. 11; Harley's Dream, p. 21; iStockphoto, pp. 13, 17, 23, 25; Shutterstock, pp. 4–5, 5, 7, 8, 9, 14, 15, 19, 20, 27, 28 (top, bottom), 29 (left, middle, right)

**Publisher's Cataloging-in-Publication Data**
Names: Olson, Elsie, author.
Title: Pet rescue / by Elsie Olson.
Description: Minneapolis, Minnesota : Abdo Publishing, 2018. | Series: Animal rights | Includes online resources and index.
Identifiers: LCCN 2017944018 | ISBN 9781532112607 (lib.bdg.) | ISBN 9781532150326 (ebook)
Subjects: LCSH: Animal rescue--Juvenile literature. | Animal rights movement--Juvenile literature. | Animal welfare--Juvenile literature.
Classification: DDC 636.0832--dc23
LC record available at https://lccn.loc.gov/2017944018

# CONTENTS

# WHAT IS
## PET RESCUE?

Do you have a friendly canine companion that greets you with a wagging tail?  Maybe you have a fuzzy cat that watches you from the window.  If so, you are not alone!

More than 65 percent of American households own a pet.  Most of these pets are dogs or cats.  More than 60 million American families have a pet dog.  And more than 47 million families have a cat.  But where do these animals come from?

Some people buy pets from pet stores or breeders.  They might also get pets from friends or family members.  But today, more and more people are adopting pets from animal shelters and animal rescues.

These organizations take in pets that don't have proper homes.  They provide food, shelter, and medical care.  Then, the shelters and rescues find safe homes for as many animals as they can.

Dogs and cats are the most common animals found in animal rescues and shelters.  But there are rescues and shelters for all kinds of pets!

# HISTORY OF CATS & DOGS

Pets have been a part of our lives for thousands of years. The first **domesticated** animal was likely the gray wolf. Scientists are not certain when or where the first domestication took place. But they believe it happened between 10,000 and 30,000 years ago. Some scientists believe wolves were domesticated at different times in different parts of the world.

How did wolves and humans become friends? Scientists think wolves started taking food from humans. In time, the wolves and humans grew less fearful of one another. Humans gave wolves easy access to food. The wolves provided protection, hunting help, and companionship. People began to breed the wolves for certain **characteristics**. Over many years, the wolves became dogs!

Researchers have compared the DNA of modern dogs with the DNA of wolves. Dogs' DNA most closely matches an extinct group of wolves from Europe!

Today, there are more than 400 breeds of dogs. The relationship between dogs and humans is like no other. Dogs can read human facial expressions in a way that no other animal can. Dogs can also be trained. Working dogs herd livestock, hunt, and even help with police work!

Cats were also **domesticated** because they were helpful to humans. Scientists believe this happened about 9,500 years ago in the Middle East. Farmers had started storing grain. Mice and other **rodents** often ate the grain.

Then, wild cats began to hunt the rodents. The cats had food to eat, and the humans no longer had pests! Modern cats are probably descended from these wild cats.

Cats have highly sensitive eyes, ears, and whiskers for tracking down rodents and other prey.

Today, cats are still mighty hunters. Many humans keep cats to help reduce rodent populations. But most owners view their cats as companions.

Cats and dogs have been popular pets for thousands of years. But animal shelters are much more recent. Around the 1700s, many towns had pounds. These places took in loose livestock.

Cats were worshipped and often mummified in ancient Egypt. They were sometimes buried with mice so they would have a snack for the trip to the afterlife!

Then the owners could pay a fee to collect their animals. However, loose dogs or cats were usually killed. They were not worth as much as horses, cows, and other livestock. People were not as concerned about animal welfare at that time.

# THE RISE OF SHELTERS

Attitudes about animals began to change in 1866. That year, the American Society for the Prevention of Cruelty to Animals (ASPCA) was formed. The ASPCA was committed to the **humane** treatment of animals. At the time, it focused mainly on protecting horses. Three years later, the women's branch of the Pennsylvania SPCA formed the Women's Humane Society. This was the first animal shelter in the country.

Animal shelters became more common over the next hundred years. In the 1930s, people began working to prevent unwanted animal births. They did this by **spaying** or **neutering** their pets. But many shelter animals were still killed due to overcrowding. In 1994, Richard Avanzino stood up against this practice.

After leading the San Francisco SPCA, Avanzino became president of Maddie's Fund. This foundation works to support the no-kill movement.

Avanzino was president of the SPCA in San Francisco, California. He wanted to end the **euthanizing** of unwanted animals. Avanzino's goal sparked a national no-kill movement. Since then, the number of animals euthanized each year has reportedly decreased by millions. There are now many shelters and rescue groups with a no-kill policy.

However, no-kill shelters fill up quickly. They must turn animals away or house them in tight spaces. Some animal **advocates** believe euthanizing is more **humane**.

# WHERE DO SHELTER ANIMALS COME FROM?

Millions of pets end up in shelters each year.  Shelter pets range from baby to elderly animals.  About 25 percent of shelter pets are **purebred** animals.  The rest are mixed breeds.

Pets end up in shelters for many different reasons.  Some are surrendered by their owners.  This may be for behavior issues.  People may realize the pet wasn't a good fit for their lifestyle.  Owners also bring in sick pets when they cannot afford to care for them.  However, most pets are surrendered because their owners are moving or not allowed pets in their home.

Not all shelter animals are surrendered by families.  Some are found wandering outside.  These animals may have gotten separated from their families.  Each year, about 710,000 stray animals are returned to their owners.

There are an estimated 70 million homeless cats and dogs in the United States.

Other animals may have never had a home. Animal control officers work for governments. They respond to requests for help with animals. These workers sometimes collect **feral** animals and bring them to animal shelters.

# PET MILLS

Some shelter pets began their lives in puppy or kitten mills. In these large breeding operations, profit is more important than animal welfare. Most mill animals are sold at pet stores.

Dogs or cats bred in mills are often crowded in unclean cages. Some spend their entire lives inside. Others are exposed to rain and snow. Pets from mills often experience lifelong health issues because of how they are bred and raised.

The government has laws for how breeders must treat their animals. Many mills break these laws. The police work with animal rights **advocates** to shut down these operations. The animals then go to shelters or rescue groups.

However, pet mills are difficult to regulate. Many operate in secret. No one knows how many pet mills exist

About 2 million puppies from puppy mills are sold each year.

in the United States.  Officials estimate there may be as many as 10,000.

It is important to remember that not all breeders run pet mills. Many breeders take excellent care of their animals.  They want the pets to go to good homes.  They will often let you come out to their businesses.  Then you can meet the animals and see how they are treated.

# ANIMAL SHELTERS

Like the animals they care for, shelters also come in many kinds and sizes.  Shelters focus on the welfare of homeless animals.  They provide medical care if needed.  They try to return lost animals to their owners.  They work to find homes for as many homeless animals as possible.

Most shelters operate on very little funding.  People must pay a fee to adopt an animal.  But this fee does not cover the full cost of the animal's care.  Shelters need government funding or public **donations** to pay for their daily operation.

There are two main types of shelters.  They are **municipal** shelters and private shelters.  Both work hard to help animals in need.

## MUNICIPAL SHELTERS

Municipal shelters are owned by the government.  They are funded by taxes.  These shelters take in all kinds of animals.

**Municipal** shelters are almost always full because they do not turn away animals. This means they are more likely to **euthanize** animals due to overcrowding. Shelters usually euthanize old, sick, and **aggressive** animals first. These animals are less likely to be adopted.

This can seem harsh to many people. But most animal **advocates** believe it is more **humane** than leaving animals to survive on their own. Without shelter, animals can starve or spread diseases.

Many municipal shelters face budget cuts and a lack of resources. This limits their abilities and the programs they offer.

# PRIVATE SHELTERS

Private shelters are funded by **donations**. These organizations can set their own policies. Some private shelters are no-kill shelters. They will turn animals away instead of **euthanizing** them. Other private shelters will not turn any animals away. They may even take in excess animals from **municipal** shelters.

The **Humane** Society of the United States (HSUS) is one of the largest private animal welfare organizations. Fred Myers co-founded the HSUS in 1954. The organization's mission is to **advocate** for the welfare of all animals.

The HSUS educates the public about animal issues. It also encourages people to adopt pets from local shelters or rescue organizations. Many cities and states also have their own humane societies. These are shelters that serve a local area. They are usually not connected to the national HSUS.

Many private shelters have support services for pet owners. They may offer a free helpline for owners to call for advice. They may also offer training classes for owners and their pets. These services make owners less likely to surrender pets during difficult times.

Many private shelters receive donations through memberships, fundraising events, and more. They can also get grants from other organizations.

# PET RESCUE GROUPS

Not all rescued pets are adopted from animal shelters. Many are adopted from pet rescue groups. Awareness of rescue groups rose with the launch of the website Petfinder.com in 1998. Thousands of rescue groups post animals for adoption on the site. Rescue groups also began to advertise on **social media** in the mid-2000s.

Rescues are usually smaller organizations than shelters. Some have their own buildings to house the animals. Others use **foster families** that take animals into their homes. These families agree to care for a homeless pet until it is adopted.

Rescues often focus on a specific type or breed of animal. Many dog rescue groups focus on greyhounds. These dogs are used for dog racing. Once they are too old to race, they are often homeless. Other rescues focus on elderly animals. You can find a rescue group for nearly any type of animal!

# RIGHTS
## SPOTLIGHT

### HARLEY, THE ONE-EYED CHIHUAHUA

Harley spent the first ten years of his life in a puppy mill. National Mill Dog Rescue saved the six-pound (2.7 kg) Chihuahua. When he was rescued, Harley was missing an eye and had a broken tail. He also had heart disease. A Colorado couple adopted Harley in 2011. To everyone's surprise, the dog recovered! In 2015, Harley was named American Hero Dog by the animal welfare organization American **Humane**. He helped encourage people to adopt dogs rescued from puppy mills.

Harley was the mascot for a National Mill Dog Rescue campaign called Harley to the Rescue.

# IS A RESCUE PET RIGHT FOR YOU?

Adopting a pet is a big responsibility. Many rescue pets come from difficult situations. This can cause behavior problems. Some also have medical problems that don't emerge until later. This can be very expensive for their new families.

Shelter workers do their best to match animals with the right families. But they often don't have time to get to know the animals. Shelters can also be **stressful** places for animals. Rescue pets may have different personalities once they leave the shelter.

Rescue organizations usually have more time to get to know their animals. **Foster families** may spend weeks or months with pets in their homes. They are more likely to notice health or behavior problems.

Some animals become shy or stressed in shelters. These animals often do better with foster families where they can receive one-on-one care.

**Foster families** can also recommend certain kinds of homes for the animals. For example, some pets do better in homes without children. Others do not get along well with other animals. This knowledge is important to consider before adopting.

Foster families and rescue groups may also interview adopters. They may ask how the adopters have prepared for a pet. Foster families and rescue groups want to make sure their animals go to happy homes.

# CHOOSING A PET

Whether you adopt from a shelter or rescue, it is important to make sure you are ready. Research the type of pet you are thinking of adopting. Choose a breed that is a good fit for your lifestyle.

You can also learn a lot from the shelter or rescue. Don't be afraid to ask questions about the animal you are adopting. Learn as much as you can about the animal's personality. If you adopt from a breeder, make sure he or she is not running a pet mill.

After you choose your pet, there will be a few costs. You will have to pay a fee to adopt the animal. This usually includes the cost of **spaying** or **neutering** your pet. But this is only a small part of the cost of having an animal. You will also have to pay for veterinary care, food, and pet supplies.

Pets can live for many years. They require lots of time and training. Are you ready to care for a pet? If you do your homework ahead of time, you will be less likely to return your new pet!

Many shelters and rescues have websites where you can see all the available animals. You should also meet your future pet in person first!

# FUTURE OF PET RESCUE

Since the 1970s, Americans have become more aware of animal welfare issues. In the 2000s, shelters and rescues began to take advantage of the Internet and **social media**. This gave them a larger audience for exposing pet mills and sharing pet stories. Today, more pets are rescued than ever before. More than 23 percent of dogs and 31 percent of cats come from animal rescues or shelters.

Animal **advocates** encourage people to adopt instead of buying from a breeder or pet store. In many communities, pet stores are not allowed to sell animals that are not from shelters or rescues. Such laws help reduce the number of pet mills. But they also hurt the businesses of honest breeders who take good care of their animals.  Because of this, not all animal **advocates** agree with these laws.

One thing all animal advocates agree on is the importance of animal welfare.  Advocates share the goal of reducing the number of homeless pets.  And thanks to hardworking people at shelters and animal rescues, that goal seems closer than ever!

Research has shown that pets are beneficial to their owners' mental and physical health!

# TIMELINE

**28,000–8000 BCE** — Dogs are domesticated from gray wolves.

**7500 BCE** — Cats are domesticated from wild cats in the Middle East.

**1866** — The ASPCA is formed.

**1869** — The women's branch of the Pennsylvania SPCA founds the country's first animal shelter.

**1930s** — People begin working to prevent unwanted animal births. They do so by spaying or neutering their pets.

**1954** — Fred Myers co-founds the HSUS.

**1994** — Richard Avanzino establishes a no-kill movement in San Francisco, California.

**2000s** — Rescue groups raise awareness of animal welfare issues through social media and the Internet.

**2015** — Harley the one-eyed Chihuahua is named American Hero Dog by American Humane.

# BECOME AN ANIMAL ADVOCATE

Do you want to become an advocate for shelter and rescue pets? Here are some steps you can take today!

**Learn about the issue.** Research animal shelters and pet rescue organizations. Learn about good breeders too. It is important to study all sides of an issue. Gather the facts and find out where you stand.

**Spread the word.** Tell your family and friends about pet rescues and other animal advocates. Encourage them to have their pets spayed or neutered to prevent future homeless animals.

**Think before getting a pet.** Research different breeds to know which ones are right for your family. Make sure you can meet the animal and ask questions before taking it home.

**Volunteer.** Most shelters and rescues take volunteers! Research organizations where you live, and find out how you can help!

29

# GLOSSARY

**advocate** – a person who defends or supports a cause.

**aggressive** (uh-GREH-sihv) – displaying hostility.

**characteristic** – a quality or feature of something.

**domesticate** – to adapt something to life with humans.

**donation** – something that is given.

**euthanize** – to kill an animal in a humane way.

**feral** (FIHR-uhl) – wild, or having gone back to an original wild or untamed state after being tame.

**foster family** – people who care for a pet in their home until the pet is adopted.

**humane** – kind or gentle to people or animals.

**municipal** – relating to a city, town, or other community with its own government.

**neuter** (NOO-tuhr) – to remove a male animal's reproductive glands.

**purebred** – an animal whose parents are both from the same breed.

**rodent** – any of several related animals that have large front teeth for gnawing. Common rodents include mice, squirrels, and beavers.

**social media** – websites or smartphone apps that provide information and entertainment and allow people to communicate with each other. Facebook and Twitter are examples of social media.

**spay** – to remove a female animal's reproductive organs.

**stressful** – full of or causing strain or pressure.

# ONLINE RESOURCES

**Booklinks**
**NONFICTION**
**NETWORK**
**FREE!** ONLINE NONFICTION RESOURCES

To learn more about pet rescue, visit **abdobooklinks.com**. These links are routinely monitored and updated to provide the most current information available.

# INDEX